SPORTS ALL-ST★RS

DANICA PATRICK

Jon M. Fishman

Lerner Publications ◆ Minneapolis

Lerner Publications Company
A division of Lerner Publishing Group, Inc.
241 First Avenue North
Minneapolis, MN 55401 USA

For reading levels and more information, look up this title at www.lernerbooks.com.

Main body text set in Albany Std 15/22. Typeface provided by Agfa.

Library of Congress Cataloging-in-Publication Data

Names: Fishman, Jon M., author.
Title: Danica Patrick / Jon M. Fishman.
Description: Minneapolis, Minnesota : Lerner Publications, [2018] | Series: Sports All-Stars | Includes webography. | Includes bibliographical references and index. | Audience: Ages: 7–11. | Audience: Grades: 4 to 6.
Identifiers: LCCN 2017035779 (print) | LCCN 2017039873 (ebook) | ISBN 9781541508507 (eb pdf) | ISBN 9781541508491 (library binding : alk. paper) | ISBN 9781541512009 (paperback : alk. paper)
Subjects: LCSH: Patrick, Danica, 1982– —Juvenile literature. | Automobile racing drivers—United States—Biography—Juvenile literature. | Women automobile racing drivers—United States—Biography—Juvenile literature.
Classification: LCC GV1032.P38 (ebook) | LCC GV1032.P38 F57 2018 (print) | DDC 796.72092 [B] —dc23

LC record available at https://lccn.loc.gov/2017035779

Manufactured in the United States of America
1-43916-33955-10/4/2017

CONTENTS

CLASH AT
DAYTONA

Danica Patrick (white car in left lane) drove one of the 17 cars on the track for the Advance Auto Parts Clash.

Danica Patrick's race car engine thundered. The bright red "10" on the car's roof was a blur as it streaked around the track. She had started the race in 12th place. But she quickly moved into fifth place. The race's leader wasn't far ahead.

Patrick was competing in the Advance Auto Parts Clash on February 19, 2017. The race was held at Daytona International Speedway in Daytona Beach, Florida. Daytona is one of the most famous racetracks in the world. It is home to some of the many **National Association for Stock Car Auto Racing (NASCAR)** events held around the world.

No woman had ever won a NASCAR race at Daytona. Patrick wanted to change that.

But 16 other drivers were trying to make sure she didn't win the race. Patrick fell back to 11th place. Then she dropped to 16th after about 35 **laps**. She was near the back of the pack, but she didn't give up. Patrick knows it takes a lot of skill and a little bit of luck to win a NASCAR race.

Patrick's car for the Clash

Patrick (*top*) needs to drive very close to other cars on the track while competing in races.

With just two laps to go, she was back among the leaders. Four cars had crashed and left the race. The remaining racers had more room on the track, so they drove faster than ever.

As they sped around a curve on the final lap, 13 cars formed a tight group. Suddenly the two leaders smashed together. Smoke from one of the cars filled the air as its tires melted on the track. It bumped into a third car, creating a shower of sparks. The lead car turned sideways and rolled to a stop. That racer's day was over.

Patrick stayed close to the outside wall to avoid the crashing cars. She sped through the smoke and drove to the middle of the track. She tried to move up, but two cars in front of her formed a wall she couldn't get past. Patrick crossed the finish line in fourth place.

She was disappointed that she didn't win the Clash. But Patrick's fourth-place finish was the best ever for a woman in a NASCAR race at Daytona. "We had a good finish and that's, at the end of the day, what we show up for," she said. Patrick will keep racing for even better results at Daytona.

The Advance Auto Parts Clash has 75 laps. Some other races at Daytona International Speedway are much longer. The Daytona 500 is the first official race of the NASCAR season. It has 200 laps.

Patrick still has the same passion for racing that developed when she was young.

Danica Patrick was born on March 25, 1982. She grew up in the village of Roscoe, Illinois. Her parents, T.J. and Bev, owned businesses in the area. Danica worked at her family's coffee shop. She didn't like the job, but she loved the village. "Roscoe was just a great place to be a kid," she said.

Danica's sister, Brooke (left), still supports her sister's racing career.

Danica was 10 and her sister, Brooke, was eight when they began racing **go-karts**. Their father set up a track in a nearby parking lot using paint cans. At first, it didn't go well for Danica. Her brakes didn't work, and she crashed into a concrete wall. "She hit the wall going about 20 miles (32 km) per hour and flipped over," T.J. said. "I thought I killed her."

She was just fine, and she loved to race. Brooke soon gave up the sport for other interests, but Danica was hooked. She began to drive against other racers her age at Sugar River Raceway in Brodhead, Wisconsin.

But soon the local tracks couldn't contain the rising star. Danica and her family traveled farther to compete against better competition. She did more than just compete—she won. Danica won the World Karting Association Grand National Championship in 1994, 1996, and 1997.

When she wasn't competing in go-karting championships, Danica was a regular teen. She was even a cheerleader in high school (*bottom right*).

Danica made the move from driving go-karts to driving formula cars as she entered the European racing scene.

In 1998, Danica and her family made a huge decision. They felt she was ready for the next level of racing. So Danica moved to England by herself. She was thrilled. "I got to leave at 16 and go live in another country away from my family and I could do whatever I wanted, and at that age that's the most exciting thing in the world," she said.

In Europe, Danica competed in full-size race cars. They had big engines in the back and fat tires that stuck out from the sides. In 2000, she finished second in the Formula Ford Festival in England. It was the best finish ever for a racer from the United States.

Danica celebrates her second-place finish at the Formula Ford Festival.

She returned to the United States in 2002 and started racing in the **IndyCar** league. In 2005, Patrick drove in the Indianapolis 500. The race, held each year in Indianapolis, Indiana, is the most famous car race in the United States. She became the first woman to ever lead the race and finished in fourth place.

Patrick was ready for a new challenge. She switched to NASCAR full-time in 2012. By then, she was one of the most popular drivers in the country. Patrick had come a long way from racing in parking lots against her sister.

Patrick waiting for her pit crew to finish working on her Indy car during the 2005 Indianapolis 500

Lyn St. James was a racing pioneer, leading the way for other young women to follow in her footsteps.

When Patrick was a teenager, she went to the Lyn St. James Driver Development Program. There, she learned more about auto racing. She found out how to make racing a career. She also learned that a successful race car driver needs to stay fit.

NASCAR races often last three hours or more. During that time, drivers don't get a chance to rest. They exit their cars at the end of a race worn out and covered in sweat. To make sure she has enough energy for the final lap, Patrick spends a lot of time working out.

Patrick usually gets up early. She exercises in the morning and sometimes in the afternoon too. CrossFit is one of her favorite workouts. It includes a variety of exercises at a fast pace: **cardio**, weight lifting, muscle stretching, and more.

Working out keeps Patrick strong for long days of racing.

Patrick shows off some yoga moves during a workout at Daytona International Speedway.

Yoga is another important part of Patrick's fitness routine. She began doing yoga in her living room as a teenager in England. It focuses on controlled body movements and breathing. Yoga helps keep her body **flexible** and her brain sharp. "I really do enjoy it," she said. "I think it's good for my body and my mind."

Healthful eating is also important to Patrick. She eats lots of vegetables and hardly ever cheats with junk food. She says that when she doesn't eat well, she doesn't feel well.

Patrick has turned her healthful lifestyle into a second job. She helped design a line of workout clothing called Warrior by Danica Patrick. The comfortable tops and stretchy pants are sold on the Home Shopping Network (HSN). She also has a book that will be released in December 2017. *Pretty Intense* is a guide to healthful eating and workouts for the body and the mind.

Patrick says she doesn't spend much time on the couch. She doesn't sit still even if she doesn't feel like a heavy workout. On those days, she does yoga or takes her dogs for a walk.

REAL-LIFE SUPERHERO

Patrick is in her element behind the wheel of a race car.

NASCAR drivers spend most of their time in the cramped cockpits of their cars. They wear bulky helmets and gear from head to toe. For some drivers, their cars are more recognizable to fans than their faces.

That's not true for Patrick. She may have the most famous face in racing. Maybe you saw her when she starred in TV commercials during the Super Bowl. Or when she appeared on TV shows such as *Today*, *The Ellen DeGeneres Show*, *The View*, and many more. She also played herself on an episode of *The Simpsons* and a fictional character on *CSI: NY*.

Patrick's fame provides lots of interesting opportunities. In June 2017, she hosted a NASCAR race from the Fox Sports television studio. She and fellow racer Denny Hamlin talked about the sport and gave their opinions of the race.

Patrick (left) guest-starred on an episode of *CSI: NY* and got to act alongside Eddie Cahill (middle) and Gary Sinise (right).

Wonder Woman

NASCAR vehicles are covered in the logos of **sponsors**. Patrick has been sponsored by companies such as GoDaddy, Monster Energy, TaxAct, and Aspen Dental.

In May 2017, Patrick drove in two races with a new sponsor painted on the outside of her car: *Wonder Woman*. She was advertising the new Wonder Woman movie that was released on June 2. The car featured images of Wonder Woman looking fierce on the sides and the hood. The hood also had two big yellow Ws that stood for Wonder Woman.

Her popularity with racing fans also helps her give back to her community. Patrick often speaks with groups of kids. She tells them inspiring stories about her life and racing. She also likes to goof off with them and have fun.

Patrick loves animals too—she has two dogs. She works with the group One Cure to fight cancer in animals. She gives money to the group and spreads the word about its work. Patrick knows that pets are important members of a family and wants to do what she can to help these furry friends.

Patrick and her boyfriend Ricky Stenhouse Jr. with their two dogs

Patrick proudly wears the One Cure logo on her racing suit.

"THE FASTEST DRIVER"

Patrick waits in her car at the start of a 2005 IndyCar race.

Danica Patrick was voted IndyCar Rookie of the Year in 2005. Since then, her racing career has included a series of firsts.

Patrick (center) on the podium after she took first in the Indy Japan 300

After being the first woman to lead the Indianapolis 500, in 2008 she became the first woman to win an IndyCar race. She crossed the finish line ahead of everyone else at the Indy Japan 300.

In 2013, she had the fastest **time trial** at the Daytona 500. That meant she would be in the **pole position** for the race—a first for a woman. She finished in eighth place.

Patrick has a great relationship with her fans. In this picture, she greets fans before a 2016 NASCAR race.

Patrick's driving skills and spirit have made her incredibly popular with fans. She was voted IndyCar's most popular driver in 2005. Then she won it every year for the next five years. She was voted most popular driver after her first season of NASCAR too.

In 2006, Patrick published an autobiography, *Danica: Crossing the Line*. Many people wait until their careers are over before writing about their lives. Patrick was just getting started. She was the first woman to reach many racing goals. But her sights are set even higher. "I was brought up to be the fastest driver, not the fastest girl," she said. "We have a lot more history to make."

Patrick presents her 2006 autobiography.

Driver	Date	Place
Sara Christian	October 2, 1949	5th place
Danica Patrick	August 31, 2014	6th place
Sara Christian	September 11, 1949	6th place
Janet Guthrie	August 28, 1977	6th place
Danica Patrick	March 29, 2015	7th place
Danica Patrick	May 10, 2014	7th place
Danica Patrick	February 25, 2013	8th place
Danica Patrick	July 6, 2014	8th place
Janet Guthrie	October 9, 1977	9th place
Janet Guthrie	October 23, 1977	9th place
Danica Patrick	April 19, 2015	9th place
Janet Guthrie	March 19, 1978	10th place
Janet Guthrie	August 22, 1977	10th place
Danica Patrick	June 4, 2017	10th place

Source Notes

8 Holly Cain, "Patrick Adds More History to Her Daytona Resume," NASCAR, February 19, 2017, http://www .nascar.com/en_us/news-media/articles/2017/2/19 /danica-patrick-daytona-clash-best-finish-by-woman.html.

9 Brant James, "Danica Patrick Has Fond Memories of Hometown," *ESPNW*, September 14, 2012, http://www .espn.com/espnw/news-commentary/article/8377897 /espnw-danica-patrick-fond-memories-roscoe-ill.

10 MB Roberts, "Danica Patrick: From Go-Kart Racer to NASCAR Contender," *American Profile*, February 8, 2014, http://americanprofile.com/articles/danica-patrick -nascar.

12 Brant James, "Danica Patrick Got Tough in England," *ESPNW*, August 29, 2013, http://www.espn.com/espnw /news-commentary/article/9612155/espnw-england -where-danica-patrick-got-tough.

17 Eve Wulf, "Behind the Body: NASCAR Driver Danica Patrick Is a Fitness Fiend," *Sports Illustrated*, July 1, 2016, https://www.si.com/edge/2016/07/28/behind-the -body-danica-patrick-workouts-fitness-crossfit-yoga.

27 Viv Bernstein, "Patrick Earns a Historic Pole, at a Premier Event," *New York Times*, February 17, 2013, http://www.nytimes.com/2013/02/18/sports/autoracing /danica-patrick-earns-pole-for-daytona-500.html

cardio: a type of workout designed to get the heart pumping and improve blood flow

cockpits: the areas where drivers sit in race cars

flexible: able to bend easily

go-karts: small, motorized vehicles for one person

IndyCar: a racing league in the United States. Indy cars have tires that stick out from the sides, and the engine is in the back of the car.

laps: complete trips around a racetrack

National Association for Stock Car Auto Racing (NASCAR): a racing league in the United States for stock cars. Stock cars look similar to cars you see on the street.

pole position: the first position at the start of a race

rookie: a first-year driver

sponsors: companies that give a race car driver money to advertise their products

time trial: a lap taken before a race to decide the order of the cars at the beginning of the race. The driver who goes fastest starts in first place.

yoga: exercises that help control the body and the mind

Anderson, Jameson. *Danica Patrick*. Minneapolis: Checkerboard Library, 2015.

IndyCar
http://www.indycar.com

Kortemeier, Todd. *Superstars of NASCAR*. Mankato, MN: Amicus, 2017.

NASCAR
http://www.nascar.com

The Official Website of Danica Patrick
https://www.danicapatrick.com

Savage, Jeff. *Auto Racing Super Stats*. Minneapolis: Lerner Publications, 2018.

Index

Photo Acknowledgments

The images in this book are used with the permission of: Jonathan Ferrey/Stringer/ Getty Images Sport/Getty Images, p. 1; Jared C. Tilton/Getty Images Sport, pp. 4–5; Chris Graythen/Getty Images Sport, pp. 6, 7; New York Daily News Archive/ New York Daily News/Getty Images, p. 9; Paul Hurley/Polaris/Newscom, p. 10; Seth Poppel Yearbook Library, p. 11; Sutton Motorsports/ZUMA Press/Newscom, pp. 12, 13; JEFF ROBERTS/AFP/Getty Images, p. 14; RacingOne/ISC Archives/Getty Images, p. 15; AP Photo/John Raoux, pp. 16, 17; Jonathan Ferrey/Getty Images Sport, pp. 19, 25; CBS Photo Archive/CBS/Getty Images, p. 20; Chris Trotman/ Getty Images Sport, p. 21; Icon Sportswire/Getty Images, p. 22; Jonathan Ferrey/ Getty Images North America, 23; Gavin Lawrence/Getty Images Sport, p. 24; Brian Lawdermilk/Getty Images Sport, p. 26; John Zissel/ZUMAPRESS/Newscom, p. 27. Design elemnts: iStock.com/iconeer (gold star); iStock.com/neyro2008 (motion lines); iStock.com/ulimi (streaked star).

Front cover: Jonathan Ferrey/Stringer/Getty Images Sport/Getty Images.